MENDED TO MEND OTHERS

From Pain to Purpose, Brokenness to Calling

Kareen Robinson

Mended To Mend Others

From Pain to Purpose, Brokenness to Calling

By Kareen Robinson

ISBN: 979-8-9955564-0-4

Publisher: Kareen Robinson

Cover design by Kareen Robinson

Table of Contents

Table of Contents 1

Dedication 3

Introduction 4

    Why This Book Exists 4

Major Loss 6

    Personal Reflection 9

Memory Loss 12

    Self-Awareness Check 15

    Reflection Questions 18

Divine Help 20

    Healing Assessment 23

New Perspective 25

    Truth Replacement 29

The Hidden Cost 31

    Scripture for Reflection 33

    Truth Revealed 34

    Reflection Questions 34

    Faith Action Step 35

Mended to Mend Others 36

Scripture for Reflection 39

Truth Revealed.. 39

Reflection Questions..................................... 40

Faith Action Step 41

About The Author... 43

Dedication

This book is dedicated to everyone who has experienced grief, hurt, pain, isolation, or abandonment, or who has been genuinely misunderstood. Remember, you are not your past, though your past has shaped your present.

You have the power within you to create a wholesome future for yourself and those you encounter, but this can only be achieved when Christ becomes your choice. His grace and mercy will transform you, enabling you not only to heal from your deepest hurts but also to guide and mentor others.

I charge you to dedicate your life to serving as Christ calls us to serve.

Introduction

Why This Book Exists

There are wounds we learn to hide so well that even we forget they are still bleeding. I was one of those people. I learned early how to be strong, how to smile through pain, and how to serve while silently shrinking.

This book was not written because my life was easy; it was written because it was not. I lost my mother on my birthday, and what should have been a day of celebration became a memorial of grief. That loss shaped how I saw myself, how I loved, how I learned, and how I believed God saw me.

But this is not just a story about loss; it is a story about restoration. It is a story about asking God for help and discovering that brokenness can become purpose.

Each chapter will share my journey. After each chapter, you will find reflection questions, scripture, or practical steps. This is intentional. I do not want you to simply read my story, I want you to examine your own. Because healing is not passive, and what God mends, He often uses to mend others.

Major Loss

My story began on the morning of my mother's passing. The fear and intensity in the air were so thick they felt tangible. I remember the way Mom gasped as she struggled to breathe. I remember how she tried to regulate herself, masking her pain long enough to hand me my birthday gift.

She was gentle. Calm. Brave even, knowing she might not see me again.

Suddenly, she screamed and began to push me away. At the time, I did not understand. Later, I realized she was trying to protect me. She did not want me to witness her final moments.

I was sent outside to play with my older siblings. Moments later, my grandmother screamed in horror. My siblings and I ran back inside. I watched as my mother's lifeless body slipped from my grandmother's arms onto the bathroom floor.

On that day, I saw everyone I loved weep. A day that was meant to celebrate life became marked by grief. Within our family, the shadow of loss covered every birthday that followed. My birthday was no longer simply my birthday; it became the anniversary of my mother's death.

For me, there was nothing to anticipate. No cheerful "Happy Birthday." No joyful "Good morning." No excitement. Joy had quietly exited my life, and a child was broken.

I will not say this was intentional. It was just how grief was being processed around me. Emotionally, I began to dread my birthdays. They became symbols of unbearable pain.

As the years passed, I experienced a depth of sorrow that words struggle to capture. I developed a strong desire to disappear, to sleep through the day and forget it existed. There was nothing to celebrate. Death had overshadowed the truth that life itself was still a gift.

Somewhere in my young mind, I translated this into something personal:

I must not be important.
I must not be worthy of love.
I must not deserve even a simple "Happy Birthday."

I was taught to be strong, to care for and celebrate others, and to quietly consider myself less. I began seeking approval to determine my worth.

As a child, I did not understand how dangerous that pattern could become. I believed that if I did more, helped more, and carried more responsibility, I would finally feel valued.

Instead, I was overlooked. The things I did

were viewed as obligations, not as expressions of care.

Mistrust slowly crept in, I began to question everything, mostly my own thoughts. Like everyone around me, I learned to mask my true feelings. I did what was expected and performed a strength that wasn't real.

My coping mechanism was avoidance, and the only way forward was to forget the past. At least, that is what I thought.

Personal Reflection

Take a moment to pause and be honest with yourself. This is a space for you to process what you have read and how it connects to your own experiences. There are no right or wrong answers, only an opportunity for truth and clarity.

Write freely and allow yourself to express what you may not have said before:

1. What part of this chapter has resonated with me the most?

____

____

____

____

____

____

2. What emotions did I feel while reading this?

____

____

____

____

____

3. What experience does this chapter remind me of?

____

____

____

____

____

____

Memory Loss

As the weight of grief grew heavier, I noticed something frightening. My mind, once sharp and eager, began to falter. My ability to read, to comprehend, to hold knowledge, slipped through my fingers like sand. School, which had been a place of achievement, became a stage for humiliation.

I went from being an "A" student, to struggling just to pass. I became the student, others whispered about, laughed at, or ignored entirely. I felt shame. I felt small. I felt broken.

For years, I carried the burden alone, thinking it was my fault; that I was stupid, incapable, and unworthy. Little did I know that my mind was responding to grief, that my memory and focus were being pulled under by unprocessed pain.

I had tried, in my own way, to erase the memory of my mother and to forget her passing. To avoid the sting of loss, I pushed aside everything that reminded me of her, even the lessons she had lovingly taught me: reading, writing, and arithmetic. In doing so, I inadvertently erased a part of myself, and my academics suffered.

Socially, I was adrift. Friends were few, and school became a place of awkwardness and distance. I ate alone and observed quietly from the shadows, never wanting to draw attention to the "weird," motherless girl.

Pets became my companions, and pain became my common language. In the quiet of that isolation, I developed an almost psychic awareness of brokenness in others; I could sense it before a word was spoken.

Life felt lonely. And in that loneliness, guilt lingered. A voice in my head whispered relentlessly:

You'll never be close to normal.
You don't deserve happiness.
Happiness is overrated, and it comes only with pain.
You'll never make a difference.
You're not worth loving.

Those voices carved themselves into my sense of self. My confidence and self-esteem eroded. Thoughts of vanishing, of escaping life entirely, became frequent visitors.

Eventually, a new coping mechanism took root: numbness. I learned to feel nothing, to become invisible, and to keep my pain private, as it felt safer that way. However, that safety came at a cost, leaving me disconnected from myself, my emotions, and life itself.

Finally, in the depths of despair, I cried out to God not for answers or immediate relief, but simply for someone to hear me, see me, and let me exist as I was: broken, scared, and invisible. I desperately needed love and belonging. I needed to be safe enough to finally feel. In that moment, for the first time, I felt a whisper of hope.

Self-Awareness Check

This section is designed to help you recognize patterns, thoughts, and behaviors that may be present in your life. Awareness is the first step toward change. What you can see, you can begin to address. Take a moment to pause and look inward. Answer honestly, without judgment or pressure.

- Do I see any of these patterns in my own life?   ☐ Yes   ☐ No

- Is there an area of my life where I have been blaming myself for something that may need compassion instead?
  ☐ Yes   ☐ No

- Have I been avoiding any emotions or truths?   ☐ Yes   ☐ No

  I have experienced a decline in focus, memory, or mental clarity after a painful event.   ☐ Yes   ☐ No

  I have gone from feeling capable or confident to feeling inadequate or "not enough."   ☐ Yes   ☐ No

- I have believed negative things about myself (e.g., "I'm not smart," "I'm not capable").
  ☐ Yes   ☐ No

- I try to avoid memories or anything that reminds me of past pain.
  ☐ Yes   ☐ No

- I feel isolated, disconnected, or like I do not belong.
☐ Yes   ☐ No

- I withdraw or stay quiet to avoid attention or judgment.
☐ Yes ☐ No

- I have experienced deep loneliness, even when around others.
☐ Yes ☐ No

- I feel overly aware of or sensitive to the pain of others.   ☐ Yes ☐ No

- I carry guilt or an inner voice that speaks negatively about me.
☐ Yes   ☐ No

- I feel like I have to handle my struggles on my own.   ☐ Yes   ☐ No

- Did this section help me see my struggles differently, not as personal failure, but as a response to pain?

☐ Yes   ☐ No

Reflection Questions

1. What is one truth I can begin to embrace about myself today that challenges the negative narrative I've carried?

2. How does recognizing the impact of grief or pain change the way I view my past?

____

____

____

____

____

3. How can I be more gentle and compassionate instead of blaming myself?

____

____

____

____

____

Divine Help

I had cried enough tears to fill oceans, yet my heart still felt heavy, burdened, and broken. That night, I did something I had never done before: I prayed with complete honesty. Not carefully. Not politely. Not with words I thought God wanted to hear. I cried. I raged. I questioned. I even challenged Him.

"If You are God," I whispered through swollen lips, "and You care for me, why haven't You helped?"

And then, almost immediately, the stillness around me shifted. A presence so warm and pure enveloped me completely. A voice, gentle yet firm, whispered inside my soul *"You asked not, so you received not. I have always been here, protecting you in ways you cannot yet imagine."*

I was stunned. No one was in the room. No one could see me, yet I felt the unmistakable touch of God's love wrapping around the deepest part of me, the little girl who had been silenced, buried beneath grief, fear, and numbness.

For the first time, I understood that I was loved; truly, unconditionally, and eternally loved. Not for what I did, how I performed, or for how strong I appeared to be. Loved simply because I existed.

I curled into that embrace as though I were an infant and I cried. But this time, the tears were tears of relief, of release, of joy I did not know I could feel. My despair was being exchanged for hope, my fear for comfort, and my heaviness for a new sense of lightness.

In that sacred moment, I realized how I had limited God. I had blamed Him, cursed Him, and doubted His care; yet He had never abandoned me. He had always been present, guiding, protecting, and loving me in ways beyond my understanding.

The experience shifted everything. I noticed the people God had placed around me: neighbors who treated me like their own family, friends who shielded me from cruelty, and a church family that welcomed me when I had nowhere else to belong.

Even as my biological family struggled with grief, God provided me with a village. He gave me a family beyond blood and a safety net I hadn't fully recognized until now.

Through this encounter, I learned the first profound truth that healing begins when we invite God into our pain and surrender to His presence. His love, unlike human love, never fails, never falters, and never abandons us.

Life was slowly becoming worth living again. Although the world still reminded me of my struggles and my scars, I carried a newfound sense of hope. When negative thoughts rushed through my mind like a runaway train, God would intervene through a song, a conversation, a gentle whisper, or even the sight of creation. He reminded me that I am loved, I am seen, and I am not alone.

In that divine love my purpose began to awaken. I began to see that the very brokenness I thought was my curse could become a source of light for others. The little girl I once held captive in silence began to emerge, stronger, wiser, and ready to step into the plan God had for her life.

Healing Assessment

Take a moment to pause and reflect. This assessment is not about judgment or right answers. It is a tool to help you become aware of where you are. Healing begins with truth. What you acknowledge, you can address.

Answer honestly based on your current experience. There is no pressure, only clarity. Some questions may feel uncomfortable, and that is okay. Discomfort often reveals areas that need healing. Use the scale below to rate each statement:

(1 = Not at all true for me, 2 = Slightly true for me, 3 = Somewhat true for me, 4 = Mostly true for me, 5 = Completely true for me)

- I feel worthy of love: _______

- I understand my past without blaming myself: _______

- I am open to healing: _______

- I believe my life has purpose: _______

New Perspective

As time passed and God's presence became a daily reality in my life, I began to see things differently. It wasn't that my family didn't love me. The truth was far more complex. They were all grieving. Each in their own way, without guidance or counsel. There were no instructions on how to cope with such immense loss, no manual for raising children while mourning a spouse.

We grieved as individuals, trying to keep life functioning. Avoidance became a way of survival. Mentioning Mom was painful, so it often went unspoken. Strength was expected, silence required. It was not ideal. It was not healthy. But it was real.

Slowly, I began to understand: my father loved me. Perhaps not perfectly, and not in the ways I wanted, but deeply. I watched him work long hours, return home exhausted, yet still roll up his sleeves, cook dinner, wash clothes by hand, and comb my hair. He checked my homework and guided my brother and me through chores. There were no complaints, no dramatic displays, just steadfast love expressed through tireless action.

Even the most mundane tasks became lessons in care and resilience. My father invited us to help him, turning responsibility into shared experiences. Sometimes it was difficult. Sometimes it was messy. But somehow, it was fun. And through it, I learned the first lesson from a true perspective: love is not always loud, and grief does not make anyone incapable of it.

I realized that every family has struggles, pain, and unspoken challenges. My family was far from perfect, yet they were functional in ways I hadn't fully appreciated. They were doing their best, and with that understanding, my heart began to soften. Resentment faded. Compassion grew.

In this newfound wisdom, I felt a stirring in my spirit. If I could understand my family's brokenness and still find love and purpose, then perhaps I could reach out to others who struggled similarly. I could extend care to those whose hearts were heavy, whose lives felt invisible. My experiences, once a source of shame and pain, became tools for empathy and service.

I dedicated myself to empowering those around me, the young and the old. It began at home: preparing meals, caring for my father, supporting my elderly uncle, helping neighbors, and even nurturing animals. I witnessed the ripple effect of small acts of love and presence. A smile returned, a burden lightened, and a moment of hope restored.

Through service, I discovered purpose. My focus shifted from my own lack to being a source of light for others. It brought me satisfaction and fulfillment deeper than anything I had experienced. What I was doing felt right; it felt pleasing to God.

After finishing college, I became a classroom teacher. I quickly realized that I could do more than teach the curriculum. I could identify the invisible barriers to learning, emotional wounds, unspoken trauma, and grief. By sharing parts of my story in age-appropriate ways, I gained my students' trust and inspired them to overcome their own obstacles.

I became a safe space, a mentor, and a guide. Christ was invited into each conversation, providing the wisdom and understanding necessary for both academic and personal growth. In these moments, I understood my calling. What God had mended in me could now be used to mend others.

Truth Replacement

Pain does not just wound; it also speaks. Over time, it can plant false beliefs that shape how you see yourself, others, and even God. If left unchallenged, those beliefs can feel true, even when they are not.

This section invites you to identify the lies you may have believed and replace them with truth rooted in clarity, understanding, and the Word of God.

Take your time. What you replace will begin to reshape how you think, respond, and live.

1. Write one negative thought you've had about yourself.

2. Now replace it with truth.

The Hidden Cost

All the joy and fulfillment I had discovered came with a price, one few people saw or understood. There were nights without sleep because God placed someone on my heart, someone who needed care, encouragement, or simply someone to listen.

The burden of obedience is heavier than most imagine. People often misunderstand compassion, seeing it as weakness. I have been called "soft" because I care for those who are neglected or forgotten.

I have been ridiculed, misjudged, and accused of being easily manipulated. Yet, the truth is that I reach people in ways that may not align with popular belief, because I meet them where they are, not where the world expects them to be.

Every person is different. Every heart is fragile in its own way. To truly reach someone, I must be patient, observant, and vulnerable. I must understand how they think about themselves, about others, and about the world. I must listen deeply, not just to words, but to unspoken truths. And that requires honesty from both sides.

This work is not easy. It is demanding. It is exhausting, yet it is my calling. I love what I do. It comes naturally because it is aligned with who I am and with who God has made me to be.

I am not immune to sin or temptation. I have struggles, moments of weakness, and times when I falter. But God has chosen me for this task. I am just a humble servant, doing His work.

At times, my life has been controversial. My methods are unconventional. My heart has offended others unintentionally. I apologize for any pain caused along the way. Yet, I continue to walk faithfully, guided by God's wisdom and empowered by His grace.

When I reflect on where I have been and where I am now, there is only one answer: Jesus, Jesus, Jesus. Thank You, Lord, for ordering my steps, guarding my heart, and strengthening my spirit and my mind. For making a way where there seemed to be no way. Thank You, Lord, for revealing Yourself unto me and opening my intellect.

To my readers, I want to leave this truth: just as God has done for me, He will do for you. His promises are sure. He is perfect. He cannot lie.

Scripture for Reflection

Jeremiah 29:11: *"For I know the plans I have for you,"* declares the Lord, *"plans to prosper you and not to harm you, plans to give you hope and a future."*

Truth Revealed

- Obedience comes with sacrifice.

- Compassion may be misunderstood, but it is never wasted.

- God equips the broken to become healers, leaders, and guides for others.

Reflection Questions

1. Where have I felt misunderstood or unappreciated because of my compassion?

2. What burdens has God placed on my heart that I may be avoiding?

____

____

____

____

3. How can I serve others without seeking approval or recognition?

____

____

____

____

Faith Action Step

Ask God to reveal where your calling intersects with service. Step forward in one small act of obedience today, trusting that He will provide strength for the journey.

Mended to Mend Others

What once broke me now equips me. Every tear, every moment of despair, every hour spent feeling unseen, it all led me here, to a place of purpose. The little girl who once believed she was invisible, unworthy, and forgotten has grown into a woman who sees others, hears them, and serves them.

I became a teacher not simply to deliver lessons from a curriculum, but to recognize the invisible barriers that hold children back. I could see the wounds behind their eyes, the weight of trauma in slouched shoulders, the quiet desperation of those yearning to be understood.

And I discovered something miraculous:

when I shared my story, my struggles, my grief, my failures, students felt safe. They felt seen. They felt hope.

Christ became the center of these moments. Through prayer, divine wisdom, and guidance, He allowed me to support my students academically, emotionally, and spiritually. The small victories, such as a student reading confidently for the first time, a tearful confession of hurt, and a smile returned after long silence, became proof that God's healing could ripple outward.

I realized the truth I had always been learning. Our pain is never wasted when surrendered to God. It is a tool, a bridge, and a lamp for others wandering in darkness. My brokenness became my ministry, and my scars became my story. My past became a guide for those walking paths I once traveled.

But this calling is not easy. It requires patience, persistence, and humility. It means showing up even when misunderstood, even when my methods are questioned, even when the world does not recognize the weight of the work being done. Yet, I cannot stop. I am compelled by love, by obedience, by the knowledge that someone, somewhere, may be mended because I dared to walk faithfully in my calling.

Through serving others, I have found purpose. Through Christ, I have found clarity. Through reflection and obedience, I have found joy. And through all of it, I have learned that life is not about perfection, accolades, or approval; it is about love expressed, wounds healed, and hope shared.

So I offer this to you, dear reader...

Your pain does not define you. Your scars do not disqualify you. God can take what was broken and use it to build strength. What you have endured can become a beacon for others. In surrender, in faith, and in service, you can be mended to mend others.

Walk boldly. Love fiercely. Serve humbly, and let your brokenness become the light that guides someone else home.

Scripture for Reflection

Psalm 147:3: *"He heals the broken-hearted and binds up their wounds."*

Matthew 5:16: *"Let your light shine before others, that they may see your good deeds and glorify your Father in heaven."*

Truth Revealed

- Healing transforms personal pain into purpose.

- Scars are not shame, they are stories that inspire others.

- Service fueled by God's love has lasting impact beyond measure.

Reflection Questions

1. How has my own pain prepared me to help someone else?

____

____

____

____

____

2. Where can I offer compassion, patience, or understanding today?

____

____

____

____

____

____

3. In what ways can I allow God to use my story to guide others?

____

____

____

____

____

Faith Action Step

Identify one person you can encourage, mentor, or support this week. Step forward with love, trusting God to use your past for their healing.

Prayer: Write a prayer based on what you need right now:

About The Author

Kareen Robinson is a compassionate educator, mentor, and faith-driven servant dedicated to helping others heal, grow, and discover their purpose. Through her personal journey of loss, grief, and restoration, she has developed a deep understanding of the emotional and spiritual challenges many face but often struggle to express.

As an educator, Kareen goes beyond the classroom, creating safe and supportive spaces where individuals feel seen, heard, and valued. She uses her life experiences to connect with others on a meaningful level, guiding them through their struggles with empathy, wisdom, and faith.

Mended to Mend Others is a reflection of her journey. A testimony of how brokenness can be transformed into purpose through Christ. Kareen believes that every person has the ability to heal and become a source of light for others when they embrace faith, truth, and love.

Her mission is to inspire, uplift, and empower individuals to walk boldly in their purpose and trust in God's plan for their lives.